MW00653615

Flowering YOUR MIND

SUZANNE FAITH

2021 Nature of Design
47 Great Western Rd, South Yarmouth, MA. *02664*
Copyright © *2021*, Suzanne Faith.   All Rights Reserved.

No part of this publication may be reproduced or transmitted in any form or by any means, electronic
or mechanical, including photocopying, recording or otherwise, without permission in writing by the
publisher or author (Nature of Design, Suzanne Faith).
First Edition *2021*
ISBN *978 0 578 84513 5*

Book illustrations: Suzanne Faith
Cover illustration: Suzanne Faith
Cover design: Taylor Baybutt

ACKNOWLEDGEMENT

I wish to express my sincere thanks to all those whose encouragement went into the completion of this book.

To Nobuo Sugino who first planted the seed of the idea.

To Chris Boyer and Beth Ann Lombardi who skillfully edited the manuscript.

To Taylor Baybutt whose artistic editorial eye guided the cover design and interior layout.

To the millions of flower lovers around the world who appreciate and understand the healing power of nature.

TABLE OF CONTENTS

PART 1: FLOWERING YOUR MIND

PART 2: FLOWERING YOUR LIFE

Part 1

FLOWERING YOUR MIND

Introduction

As we search for quality and balance to our lives, finding ways to reduce stress and improve cognitive function are becoming increasingly more important to us. For many, especially those in the baby boomer generation, we have seen how advancing age and loss of memory can quickly create a situation of dependency and decline. Recommendations ranging from exercise and Mediterranean diets, to crossword puzzles and coloring books seem to pop up daily in the search to keep our minds active and our brains stimulated. But what if you were to find out that the simple addition of flowers into your life could improve your cognitive health as well as enhance your sense of well-being?

For centuries plants and their flowers have been the basis of remedies found in essential oils, tonics, and teas used to heal the body. Plants provide us with everything from food, clothing, and shelter, to medicine and oxygen. Remarkably, it is now evident that the brain's response to the beauty of flowers provides yet another powerful gift: *flowers can actually improve emotional health and cognitive function, especially when combined with some form of creative expression.* Given today's increasing number of stress-related disorders, dementia, and aging baby boomers, perhaps the benefits of adding flowers to one's life holds at least one of the keys to maintaining a healthy, stimulated brain.

Flowering Your Mind combines research with practical suggestions and ideas to help you fully understand the flower-brain connection and learn to reap the cognitive and emotional benefits of creatively incorporating flowers into your life.

My Personal Connection to Flowers

As far back as I can remember, my experience with flowers has been an important and far-reaching part of my life. Flowers, with their endless variety of shapes and colors, never ceased to engage my curiosity and offered me the perfect medium to engage my creative expression. The world of gardening exposed me to a vast array of flowers and botanicals, which allowed me to explore and make sense of the world around me. I credit my deep interest in flowers to my mother and my grandmother, who taught me how to plant and nurture gardens filled with color. From the age of three, my playground was the wild, wild fields, and when our neighbor introduced me to the world of flower pressing at the age of eight, I felt an immediate connection to the flowers with which we worked. She showed me how to select and ready specimens for pressing in the tissue-thin pages of a telephone book and how, after a few weeks, the flowers could be used in a variety of craft projects.

As a teen, my creative expression shifted to the art of fine line pen and ink illustrations. Using a drafting pen, I lost myself by immersing my imagination in the miniature detailed worlds I created on paper. This need to express myself through creating became integral to my being, and while I wanted desperately to go to art school, my parents, both teachers by profession, could not see the logic of this as a career. Instead they encouraged me to study nursing, and although I agreed, I often struggled to find my creative voice in a world governed by strict parameters and guidelines.

Clarity finally came to me during my psychiatric clinical rotation, during which the study of the brain and human behavior piqued my interest. I began to notice the therapeutic value that drawing and painting had on the emotional healing of some of my clients. I began to understand that creating, regardless of the medium, offered a healthy way to release energy and express emotion. In short, I saw that when words fail, creative expression could take its place.

Over the years I have used my degree to specialize in the field of dementia, and have gained experience using creative activities to decrease anxiety and stress in the individuals with whom I work. My own artistic endeavors have continued as well, and I have discovered ways to combine my love of flowers with my love of pen and ink illustrations. My roles as both psychiatric nurse and artist have provided me with unique opportunities to navigate both the medical and creative communities. This in turn has provided me with a deeper understanding of the role creative expression has on the brain and the power certain visual symbols, such as flowers, can have on stimulating the mind.

As a member of the Pressed Flower Guild of Great Britain I had the opportunity to travel to England to learn their well-established pressing methods. The English are purists and very traditional when it comes to this craft. As such, they considered my designs, which combine pen and ink illustrations with pressed flowers, a bit unconventional. The Japanese, on the other hand, were intrigued by this combination of mediums and invited me as a member of the International Pressed Flower Art Society to their country to teach.

While in Japan I was introduced to the word *Oshibana*, which means pressed plant, and the term *Oshibana Therapy*, which refers to the practice of working with pressed flowers to provide a sense of well-being. Simply put, when the body is in a state of stress, blood vessels constrict, slowing the flow of blood through the body and reducing the amount of energy and oxygen moving through the cells. The brain's response to the visual beauty of flowers helps to relax and open the body's circulatory system, thus releasing stress and tension that has built up in the cells. Creating designs with pressed flowers, *Oshibana Therapy*, is believed to decrease many conditions that are brought on by stress and negative emotion such as ulcers, migraines, stomach distress, high blood pressure, and depression. Stress collects in our cells and over time; if left unchecked, it can lead to serious health problems. It has been found that the positive influence of flowers in our lives can be a strong counterbalance to the negative energy that stress produces in our bodies. It does not matter whether you surround yourself with flowers in nature, observe them in an arrangement or go one step further and actually create artful designs with flowers. The visual impact flowers have on the mind enables our senses to release a positive flow of emotions.

Increasingly, research is revealing that simply being with or looking at plants and flowers can contribute to our physical, mental, and emotional health. According to behavioral research conducted by Jeanette Haviland-Jones at Rutgers University, 98% of the population experiences happy, positive emotions from the presence of flowers (Jeanette Haviland-Jones, 2001). Being in a room with a beautiful floral arrangement can brighten your mood, relieve tension, and even change the course of your day.

I believe that flowers exist in our physical world as messengers for healing our spirits and engaging our minds. ***Flowering Your Mind*** provides you with context and perspective that will soon have you gazing at these wonders of nature in a whole new way!

Chapter One

CREATIVITY AND HEALTH

THE IMPORTANCE OF A CREATIVE LIFE

The need to create is universal. It exists within each of us no matter what medium is chosen for expression. While many consider the act of *creating* in terms of the artist who takes raw materials and is able to combine them to form beautiful works of art, creative expression encompasses so much more. Chefs who take simple ingredients and create gourmet meals, or teachers who masterfully transform concepts into class lessons are also are participating in the act of creating.

Engaging in *any* form of creative expression awakens and stimulates our senses to work in unison. When we create, every cell in our brain and our body reacts to incoming sensory information. Our brain starts talking to itself. Our internal communication network is triggered and comes alive with a flood of energy and activity as sensory information begins to move. This energy that is sparked through the flow of creative expression, through each thought and action, is the same energy that connects us to the very essence of being alive.

The root of the word "create" means to bring forth into existence. The energy that moves through us while we create is called our true self, our spirit, and the feelings it stirs in us we call emotion. E-motion means just that—energy that is in motion running through our body. In a way, it is our emotions that form the bridge between our mind and body.

The expression of being "in the zone" is the feeling we have when our mind and body are connected in a singular process. This feeling, this emotion we experience when we are in process of creating, forms the link that allows our energy to flow from our spirit to our mind and through our body. This connection is what allows us to *bring forth from concept into existence*. Energy moving through the body stimulates the release of emotion, which helps to reduce stress and promote well-being. When we are doing what we love, and loving what we do, our vitality and zest for life is at its peak.

Although it may not always be clear where our creativity lies, we often know when we are feeling creative. The mind becomes sharp and ideas seem to flow effortlessly. It's important to expand our definition of what it means to be creative. Creating is a process that ignites the mind and brings forth into our world something that was not there before. Using the imagination to engage in creative thinking is just as much a process of creating as putting a paintbrush to a canvas. Creating helps to jumpstart the brain and teaches us how to connect to ourselves.

We are all born to be creative and to find innovative and useful patterns that help us navigate our lives. Adding even a small amount of creativity can help us to feel more alive. Creating and being connected to the source of our creativity is available to each and every one of us; we just need to be still enough to listen. Trying something new or something old in a brand-new way; slowing down perceptions and allowing time to savor them; and opening the senses to guiding the imagination are just a few examples of how we can better connect as sensory beings living a physical world.

THE INTERSECTION BETWEEN CREATIVITY AND THE BRAIN

Recently there has been increased interest in understanding how engaging in creative endeavors seems to improve cognitive performance. Using advanced neuroimaging, scientists are able to see the creative process in action. Multiple areas of the brain connect as they become stimulated simultaneously during the act of creating. New and alternative neural pathways are formed as information is observed moving through the brain. Multiple intersecting pathways connect various regions of the brain, forming the necessary links to evoke memories, tap into motor skills, and revive the senses, awakening the brain to work in harmony.

Listening to an old musical favorite can cause us to remember not only the words to the song, but also who we were with, what we were doing, and even the smell of the food or the weather. All of these senses, which have been stored in different areas of the brain, awaken in a single moment simply by hearing the song. As the brain works to recreate the experience of a particular moment in time, cognition and a sense of well-being are also improved. Understanding how sensory experiences stimulate these connections in the brain can provide opportunities to consciously strengthen the internal communication system in our brains.

In light of this new understanding, neuroscientists at universities across the country and around the world have been exploring the use of creative expression as a powerful tool to impact the stimulation and creation of new neural networks in our brains. Since the communication system within the brain operates on the strength of these neural networks, the more pathways we create, the greater the capacity we have to connect to new experiences with memory data that has previously been stored. The formation and strengthening of new neural networks help preserve the brain's ability to communicate within itself and build reserves. Research findings on creativity and Alzheimer's disease suggest that individuals who have continued to challenge themselves mentally over the years have stronger and more numerous neural networks, which may help to delay the onset of the disorder in those who are at risk for it.

As the baby boomer population ages and people in general are living longer, the search for ways in which to help preserve and maintain cognitive status is increasing, focusing on the desire to continue enjoying physical and mental wellness. The general advice, "use it, or lose it," includes recommendations ranging from engaging in an aerobic activity for at least thirty minutes three to four times a week, to challenging one's self with the mental the activities of crossword puzzles or Sudoku, or even learning a new language or skill.

The popularity of coloring books, with designs to color for any skill set and interest is evidence that the concept of creative expression is going mainstream. Coloring is marketed as a way to become mindful, to be in the moment, which allows the stress of the day to melt away. While this is true, the motor skills used to color, and the choices of color one decides to use, as well as the design one is coloring, all have an effect on sensory information going into the brain. This is another example of how engaging in a simple creative exercise can help link multiple areas of the brain to work together.

Exploring new skills or various modes of creative expression may not only help improve one's mental capacity, but it may also hold the key to working successfully with those who have memory impairment. Every day, our brain receives and processes thousands of sensory signals that help us interpret our experiences in the world. What we see, taste, smell, hear, and touch at any given moment is what creates the experience, while our brain decides whether it wants to store the experience for future reference. The smell of fresh baked bread or chocolate chip cookies can elicit a flood of memories that call the brain to attention. The color combination of red and green forever reminds us of Christmas, just as hearing a long-forgotten song can transport us back in time. These are sensory experiences that have been stored and can be reawakened through re-exposure to the original sensory stimulus that created them.

CREATING FOR EMOTIONAL HEALTH

Studies show that the act of creating not only increases the circulation and stimulation of neural pathways in the brain, but also that this stimulation has a positive effect on mood and morale. Stress causes the blood vessels in the brain to constrict, decreasing circulation and blocking the flow of energy. Think of a writer or artist expressing that they have writer's block or creative block. The body senses this change and signals to other parts of the body tighten, blocking energy flow. This results in a state of disease. Creativity opens up the flow of blocked energy, returning the body to a more natural, harmonious state.

According to Gene D. Cohen, M.D., Ph.D. in his book *The Creative Age: Awakening Human Potential in the Second Half of Life* (Gene D. Cohen, 2000), creativity improves life in a variety of ways. Engaging in creative endeavors fosters a sense of well-being, which boosts the immune system and contributes to overall health. Creating promotes the release of positive emotions through the parasympathetic nervous system while decreasing the flow of negative emotions. Creating also requires the hands to coordinate a large variety of fine motor movements. These movements, along with the increased use of hand-eye coordination, stimulate the visual spatial centers of the brain. The more the brain is able to communicate in unison with all its parts, the more pronounced the sense of harmony.

Science has now confirmed that creative expression is an important adjunct to overall brain health. A healthy brain helps to maximize our capacity to deal positively with our environment, promoting health and wellbeing. Creative expression empowers us and enables us to connect and discover our true self through self-expression. Candace Pert, a biophysics and physiology professor at Georgetown University Medical Center, has extensively studied the impact of creativity on the brain. Her research (Candace Pert) suggests the existence of a two-way communication link between the brain and the immune system with each influencing the other. She theorizes that the emotional connection one experiences while creating actually causes the brain and the immune system to release a series of neuro-chemicals throughout the body, which promote health and well-being.

There are a lot of misconceptions about what it takes to express oneself creatively. Some believe people are either born with talent or not. Many are afraid of playing with creative expression since they are afraid they lack talent. They fear they won't "do it right" and will therefore gain no benefit from engaging in a creative activity.

What's important is that engaging in any activity that allows a flow of creative expression provides a distraction for the brain while providing a break from the usual daily thoughts. The average person has 60,000 thoughts per day, and 95% of them are exactly the same day in and day out (Truth Inside of You). This repetition of thought does nothing to stimulate or build new neural pathways.

Creating consciously and with intention allows the creative process to be the healer, as the brain and body are stimulated to work together as one. The physiology of the body changes from one of stress to one of relaxation. There is a reason you feel "in the zone" when you become totally immersed in a creative activity. The brain wave patterns this type of engaged activity produces causes the autonomic nervous system to flood the brain with an increase in positive, stimulating neurotransmitters. Blood flow not only increases to the brain but to the entire body, nourishing the cells with oxygen and creating a healing physiology.

Healing comes from within as our creative self takes us on the journey inward, opening up our imagination and connecting us to our innermost emotions. The journey inward is to that of our very spirit—that which animates us and flows through us as our vital life force. In order to create, the mind and body must work in unison. They are not separate, but rather extensions of one another. That which forms the bridge weaving these two energetic forces together is our emotions creating an interdependent and interconnected system. Cultivating the ability to create consciously affords us the opportunity to become whole, brings us clarity of mind, and rewards us with emotional well-being.

Chapter Two

FLOWERS: NATURE'S GIFT TO OUR HEALTH

HOW FLOWERS AFFECT EMOTION

Emotions are stored in the memory along with the events that triggered those emotions. If a memory of an event triggers a happy response, our brains will subconsciously guide us back to that feeling of being happy whenever we encounter a similar event. By immersing ourselves in creative activities that are connected to positively charged memories and emotions, we can guide our minds to become our own inner healer, enabling us to improve our health and sense of well-being.

To achieve emotional well-being it is important to understand where feelings come from and how they relate to the mind and body. In *Molecules of Emotion* (Candace Pert) Dr. Candace Pert documents the research she conducted at the National Institutes of Health (NIH) and her discovery that there is a biochemical trigger in the brain that causes emotion to be expressed. The trigger, in this case, are chains of peptides-amino acids which become activated through sensory experiences. These peptides exist in our brains and throughout our entire body. Based on the strength of a sensory experience, the body knows how much more or less peptide to produce. The body responds to the release of these peptides by creating a series of internal feedback loops, which help us to feel a sense of wholeness and well-being internally. Understanding this system provides the ability to consciously create by exposing oneself to positive sensory stimuli.

The natural world is filled with a multitude of sensory stimuli, some positive, some not. Man's ability to respond and be restored by nature is well documented. Just as a phobia relates to a fear of something, a philia is an affinity towards something. The term biophilia was first used by Erich Fromm (Fromm) to describe the inherent inclination of humans to affiliate with plants, nature, and other living things. This connection between man and nature exists in our subconscious mind. It influences various regions of the brain reducing stress, and improving attention and overall physical health. Research on biophila (Patil) suggests these effects occur largely because nature, whether consciously or unconsciously, is simply pleasing to the eye.

Since the speed of light is faster than sound, our brains process visual inputs faster than anything else. Our eyes receive images in the form of light density, causing the retina to send that information to the brain, which then processes shape, color, and orientation of what it is seeing.

According to Mary Potter, Professor of Psychology, Emerita., Department of Brain and Cognitive Sciences at MIT in Cambridge, Massachusetts, and senior author of a study published in 2014 in the journal *Attention, Perception, and Psychophysics* (Potter), the human brain has the ability to interpret images that the eye sees in just thirteen milliseconds. This would indicate that the eye finds concepts and the brain responds before it actually defines what it is looking at. Based on the context of where the image is seen, this can cause the brain's immediate interpretation of a long, straight structure lying on the ground to be a stick, where upon closer inspection it is actually a snake.

With our affinity towards the natural world, simply seeing the positive visual images of nature will trigger a release of positive memories and emotions throughout the body. Research has confirmed that flowers, as representations of the natural world, create a unique and powerful stimulus in the brain. Test subjects who were shown flowers demonstrated an increase in the electromagnetic energy circulating through their brains. When there is an increase of positive flowing energy through the body, there is improved physical, mental, and emotional health.

Of all the available creative tools, flowers are by far the most powerful visually stimulating images. Whether painting, arranging, or growing flowers, or keeping a continued display of them in our living space, one could say that flowers are a gift nature has given us to manage stress naturally in our everyday lives.

For quite some time now the scientific and medical communities have been presenting surprising research revealing the many ways flowers can affect our health and happiness. Historical records show that the first hospitals in Europe were infirmaries in monastic communities where gardens were considered an essential part of the environment that supported the healing process. In 1768, Dr. Benjamin Rush, a signer of the Declaration of Independence, documented that gardening improved the condition of mentally ill patients (Eva C. Worden). Even Florence Nightingale, when writing her *Notes on Nursing* in 1859 (Nightingale), acknowledged the beauty of nature in its "variety of form and brilliancy of color in the objects presented to patients are an actual means of recovery."

Much research has now been conducted examining the link between healing, emotional well-being, and plants. The results of these studies have all produced positive results reinforcing the idea that access to nature aids in healing. Dr. Roger Ulrich, an environmental psychologist at Texas A&M University, conducted at least twelve scientific studies to demonstrate that "just looking at certain types of everyday nature is quickly effective in producing a mild, open-eyed relaxation response" (Ulrich, View Through a Window May Influence Recovery from Surgery). In this 1984 study, Dr. Ulrich was able to confirm that when plants were visible, stress levels were reduced, the need for pain medications decreased, hospital stays were shorter, and the sense of optimism and physical well-being increased. This study, as well as his many others, forms the basis of Dr. Ulrich's book ***Theory of Supportive Design*** (Ulrich, 1997), which has become influential as a guide for creating successful healthcare facilities.

As a result of Dr. Ulrich's work, a new approach to hospital environments emerged with the creation of patient-friendly health care facilities that feature nature views for those in hospital. Plants and flowers are now regularly included among these facilities to assist in the patient healing and recovery. Park and Mattson (Seong-Hyun Park) brightened hospital rooms with flowers and plants to confirm, once again, the positive effects plants have in aiding in recovery from abdominal surgery.

With today's high-tech and fast-paced lifestyle taking its daily toll on all our lives, experts advise exercise and other personal lifestyle changes to relieve stress. Jeannette Haviland-Jones, Ph.D., a professor of psychology at Rutgers University Human Development Lab, decided to research whether flowers actually make people happy.

In 2001 she combined efforts of her team at Rutgers University with The Society of American Florists to conduct The Flowers & Seniors Study (Jeannette Haviland-Jones). This study set out to document the effects of flowers on older adults who are at risk of becoming less sociable and more depressed over time. The study enrolled 100 seniors, some of whom received flowers and others who did not. The results shed new light on how nature's support system helped seniors cope with the challenges of aging. Specifically, 81% of seniors who participated in the study reported a reduction in depression following the receipt of flowers. Forty percent of seniors reported broadening their social contacts beyond their normal social circle of family and close friends. And, 72% of the seniors who received flowers scored very high on memory tests in comparison with seniors who did not receive flowers.

The study raises the question of whether the flowers simply cause a change in mood, which affects motivation, and, in turn memory, or whether the flowers cause an actual change in memory function. In 2005, armed with increasing evidence of how flowers affect mood, Haviland-Jones published her extensive study on flowers and their effect on emotion in *Evolutionary Psychology* under the title: "An Environmental Approach to Positive Emotion: Flowers" (Haviland-Jones). In three separate studies, Haviland-Jones showed that flowers are indeed a powerful positive emotion inducer.

In the first study it was noted that every time a woman was presented flowers, she elicited what is known as the Duchenne, or true smile. The Duchenne smile is associated with the raising of the cheeks and crinkling around the eyes. Such a smile has been linked to positive emotion and related changes in the brain. The participants in the study who received flowers not only reported being happy, but also the effects of their happiness lasted up to three days. It was reported that those participants in the study who received candles instead of flowers as gifts did not display the Duchenne smile nor did they express any feelings of position emotion.

In the second study, Haviland-Jones's team handed out flowers or pens to riders in an elevator. People who received flowers broke the usual elevator behavior of quietly staring at the movement of the changing numbers and instead moved closer to the middle of the elevator, smiled the Duchenne smile of true enjoyment, and even initiated conversation. That effect was not seen when people were given pens. Once again, flowers elicited more positive social behavior than other stimuli.

In her third study, Haviland-Jones had her team present flowers to participants 55 years and older. This study also reported increases in positive mood and emotions. The episodic memory of the participants also improved, as they were able to demonstrate an increase in the ability to remember the details of autobiographical events in their life.

The long-term positive benefits of flowers on mood are interconnected with the positive effects they have on reducing stress and providing us with a sense of well-being. Multiple research data has been collected over the years documenting decreased stress, improved mood, faster healing post-operatively, improved socialization, and improved **performance** in offices when people are placed in proximity to flowers and plants. In 2004, Shubata and Suzuki (S. Shibata) published their study on the effects of an indoor plant on creative task performance and mood. Their study also yielded positive results on the effects of plants.

Taken together, these studies and others offer an alternative to individuals looking to manage their day-to-day moods in a healthy and natural way, and to improve the stimulation of their brains in the process.

OSHIBANA THERAPY

Flowers are beautiful expressions of nature and representations of the universal life source that connects all living things. For centuries, cultures around the world have celebrated the beauty of flowers by creating intricate garlands, arrangements, and gardens. In Japan, the art of Oshibana uses flowers that are pressed to create beautiful design work.

In 2001, NHK TV in Japan broadcast a television documentary on Dr. Koichi Hirata as he conducted his research on the brain's connection with flowers (Hirata). As a professor of neurology at Dokkyo University School of Medicine in Japan, Dr. Hirata wanted to understand how flowers activate the brain, balance the autonomic nervous system, stabilize blood pressure, and strengthen immunity. To gain this understanding he conducted his experiments while having his participants' brains viewed under light topography neuroimaging, or what is more commonly known as a PET scan.

His first experiment used neuroimaging to measure the circulation of blood through the brain when the participants created pictures using Oshibana or pressed flowers. The premise was that if simply visualizing flowers can stimulate brain activity and improve brain function, then would creating with the positive imagery of flowers cause an additional increase in brain stimulation, and would this be enough to improve memory?

The first experiment used two housewives who only had minimal experience designing with pressed flowers. They were asked to choose their favorite flowers and press them for the experiment. Dr. Hirata measured the blood flow through their brains with a PET scan. If blood flow to the brain were to increase, then specific areas on the right and left side of the brain would turn red.

The results of this experiment showed only mild to moderate changes in brain stimulation as evidenced by observing the changes in the color red during neuroimaging when participants simply looked at flowers or watched others creating with pressed flowers. However, when the two participants actively engaged in creating their own pressed flowers pictures, the test areas marking brain stimulation turned completely red. Dr. Hirata's research concluded that creating with flowers had a greater impact on brain circulation than did simply observing an activity using flowers. This increased circulation also had a secondary effect on the participants of activating overall brain functioning and stimulating positive emotions.

Dr. Hirata's second experiment set out to learn if the increase in brain circulation and blood flow caused by creating with flowers also helped to improve memory. Participants in this experiment first took a simple memory test asking them to choose ten playing cards and recall the details of these cards after 30 minutes. The results were documented. The participants then spent the next five days creating Oshibana pressed flower pictures. After five days, they were asked to once again choose ten playing cards and recall the details after 30 minutes. The experiment documented an improvement of the number of cards recalled after spending five days creating pressed flower pictures.

Dr. Hirata concluded that the improvement in memory was directly related to increased brain activity occurring while creating with flowers. Designing with pressed flowers not only stimulated the creative expression on the right half of the brain, but also activated the areas of the brain where fine motor movement and spatial relationships reside in the parietal lobe. When the entire brain is activated simultaneously, the overall flow of energy moving through the brain improves memory, recall, and emotional well-being.

A simple way to improve our emotional health is to create with flowers. When we create, the communication system in the brain becomes activated, stimulating the flow of energy throughout the body. We now know that we can boost that flow of energy by creating with visual images to which the brain responds positively. When the nervous system is stimulated by creative expression, such as working with flowers to create art, our life force, or energy, begins to flow more easily through us. Designing with flowers, whether in creating Oshibana pressed flower pictures, flower arranging, or gardening, can assist us in opening these channels of energy and promote an enhanced state of health and well-being. Given the increasing number of Alzheimer's cases and an aging population, plant and flower therapy will be one possible link for scientists to explore in their search for ways to guide individuals towards activities that stimulate brain circulation and connect to the network where memories are stored.

Chapter Three

CREATING WITH COLOR

COLORING OUR EMOTIONS

Flowers appear to have both immediate and long-term effects on emotional reactions, mood, social behaviors, and memory for both males and females. Just seeing the image of a flower acts as a positive stimulus for the brain, rewarding it by producing a rapid flood of positive emotions. By choosing to work with specific colors of flowers, we can create an added boost to the effect flowers produce in the brain.

Many ancient cultures used the power of sunlight and color to heal. Sunlight may seem to have no direct connection to the use of color as a mode of healing, until we consider that sunlight, when reflected through a prism, splits into all the colors of the spectrum. Color is formed when light vibrates at a certain frequency. Therefore, color, as a manifestation of light, holds a therapeutic as well as divine meaning for many cultures.

Healing temples built by the Egyptians were designed in such a way that the sunlight entering the room could be directed to shine through colored gems. This system allowed for the various colors of the spectrum to be disseminated depending upon the illness and what color was needed to heal.

Since light is energy and color is formed by light vibrating at different frequencies, one begins to understand that different colors associate with different vibrational energy patterns. This is the theory behind the practice of using color to heal.

Sanskrit writings dating back to *1800* BC describe the human body as having an invisible system of spinning wheels of energy known as chakras, which are distributed along the base of our spine to the crown of our head. Their function is to connect various physiological and neurological systems in the body. Each of these wheels or chakras vibrates to its own unique frequency and color. Knowing which chakras vibrate to which colors allows one to choose specific colors to create with, which in turn will effect or stimulate the corresponding chakra directing healing energies to be transmitted to the specific part of the body. When Chakras are open, the flow of energy is moving freely along the spinal cord uniting our physical, mental, emotional, and spiritual bodies. It is believed that clairvoyant people have the ability to see these chakras and auras when they look at the physical body.

Each individual chakra is linked directly to specific functions in the body. The colors associated with each chakra point align in accordance with the same progression of the colors seen in a prism or rainbow. The first chakra vibrates to the color red, the second to orange, the third to yellow, the fourth to green, the fifth to blue, the sixth to indigo, and the seventh to violet.

For example, when our eye sees the color red, the energy in our first chakra becomes ignited. The Chakra "wheel" begins to spin sending waves of vitality and warmth throughout our body. The retina in the human eye has the most receptors for the color red. It directs our attention and causes us to become alert. Traffic stop signs are red for this reason, as are the flashing lights on an ambulance. The stimulating effect of the color red causes the brain to become alert and aware while activating the first chakra point in the spine. The color red can help us to feel grounded and connect us to the earth energy.

Over time, red has also taken on the symbolic meaning of passion. This probably has more to do with the fact that red is the color of blood, the life force within each of us. In most cultures, red is regarded as a positive, life-giving color, especially in China where it represents luck as well as strength and masculinity. Those that are attracted to the color red are thought to be open minded and uncomplicated in nature, while those lacking this personality trait can add strength to their life by surrounding themselves with the color red until they gain the balance they were seeking.

Thus, during the creative process it is possible to alter the intention of the creation by choosing specific colors with which to create. The color red can be used as a focal point in an illustration or floral arrangement to draw the eye inward. Likewise, an entire design can be created using various hues of red, which certainly helps to ground and focus your attention while you are creating. Red flowers such as roses, poppies, dahlias, tulips, and amaryllis are perfect for creating fresh floral arrangements, but none of these flowers press well. Better choices for a pressed floral design include red verbena, salvia, crimson clover, or phlox. Not all red flowers when pressed retain their brilliant hue, and many artists use color inks and pastels to reestablish the desired shade of red color. Still others buy pressed flowers directly from online sources where many of the flowers have been permanently died to retain their color.

The second chakra is represented by the color orange. Orange is not a primary color, but rather a combination of red and yellow, often combining the qualities of each. It represents the energy of physical vitality and stimulates intellectual activity. Since the second chakra, represented by the color orange, lies in the seat of reproduction, one can begin to understand that the visual association to the color could also energize feelings of sexuality and play. Orange flowers are said to promote the healing of reproductive disorders. In various cultures around the world the color orange is also associated with eliciting feelings of strength, fearlessness, curiosity, and restlessness.

Alone, the color orange is very stimulating so often just a little touch is needed to add interest and "pop" to a creation, whether it is a design work or an outfit. The known visual stimulation caused by orange has proven a successful addition to street signs and industrial workplaces to indicate a hazardous situation. Athletes often use a florescent high-intensity version of orange to warn drivers of their presence.

Orange adds a bit of warmth to cool colors and its complementary color is blue. This should be considered when deciding on a color scheme; however, if drawn to surrounding yourself with orange you may need the invigorating qualities associated with the colors red and yellow as well. Orange has a fun-loving side, and its stimulating quality can be good for lively social conversation and good-natured humor.

Orange flowers come in many shapes and sizes, from tiger lilies, dahlias, and Gerber daisies, to pumpkin-hued roses, orchids, and calla lilies, providing many options for gardens or floral arrangements. For flower pressing, some of my personal favorites include coreopsis, some varieties of potentilla, orange poppies, marigolds, and nasturtiums, as well as many species of fall leaves gathered at their peak. Since the color orange is playful, a sense of curiosity is suggested in choosing shapes and out-of-the-ordinary combinations.

The solar plexus is the seat of the third chakra. It vibrates to the color yellow. As another of the stimulating colors, yellow is thought to enhance intellectual and mental activities. In almost every culture yellow as representative of the sun brings about brightness and creativity and humor to those it attracts. Whereas red tends to root us and ground us in the physical, the role of the third chakra, located between the navel and solar plexus, is the core of our personality, our identity, and our ego. While the sacral chakra seeks pleasure and enjoyment, the third chakra is all about the perception of who you are. Some people are described as having a "sunny" disposition. The third chakra is the center of self-esteem, willpower, and self-discipline, as well as warmth of personality.

Too much yellow can create a strong negative reaction, but for someone or something that needs brightening or lightening up, yellow can provide a bit of sunshine and warmth to an otherwise dark room or boring arrangement. Just as in anything, balance is important, and it is important to remember that too much yellow in any design can be over-stimulating. The complementary color to yellow is violet. Today, many species of flowers are bred to bloom in specific colors and yellow flowers are no exception. Look for yellow flowers whose shape and size will complement your arrangement. Day lilies, sunflowers, marigolds, snapdragons, and roses alone or in combination will create a beautiful bouquet. For pressed flowers, daffodils, daisies, golden rod, basket of gold, gaillardia, and even scotch broom can add interest as well as a bit of vibrancy to the design.

Moving up the spine, the fourth chakra is located at the level of the heart and vibrates to the color green. It is connected to love and compassion. When you look at sunlight as it moves through a prism, green is the color found in the middle of the spectrum at the midpoint between light and dark. Green is formed by mixing yellow, representing brightening and opening, with blue, representing calm and compassion. Green can open the heart to feelings of compassion and create awareness and sensitivity to the natural world. If you have ever sat in a wooded forest or gazed out on a field of green you have probably felt the soothing effect the color green has on the emotional state.

Most green-colored flowers available for flower arranging have been dyed or grown as particular hybrids to achieve their color, among them chrysanthemums, daylilies, zinnias, dianthus, Bells of Ireland, and roses to name a few. There are also many species of hydrangeas that produce a green flower and look striking in an arrangement. For a pressed floral design, I prefer to use foliage to add an overall green color to my arrangements. The silver-green foliage of dusty miller and Artemisia has particularly long-lasting color that does not seem to fade with time. As with all flowers, look for specimens that have interesting shapes to add interest to your overall floral design. Purple is opposite green on the color wheel. Placing these two colors together can create a complementary composition that is balanced in vibrational tone. Just a few splashes of purple in an otherwise green arrangement can add interest, keep the eye's attention, and provide focus.

Blue is the color that vibrates to our fifth chakra, which is located at the level of the throat. When the chakra wheel is open and spinning, we are said to be able to speak our truth. When the eye perceives color, we are actually seeing light that is reflected from that object. Visible light is just a small part of the spectrum of radio waves, which vary in length and speed. Red has the slowest and longest waves, whereas the blues and violets are shorter waves and vibrate faster. Colors that vibrate on shorter wavelengths tend to be more calming and soothing, helping us to concentrate better.

Though blue is often associated with calm and cool, blue can also be linked to feeling depressed or lonely, as in "the blues" in music, or feeling "blue." It can be said, however, that people often gravitate to a particular color because that is what they feel they are lacking in their lives. For example, if one is feeling depressed or lonely, more blue color may be desired to help create calm and stabilize emotions.

Blue is the favorite color of most people the in the world (Wolchover). The color blue represents complete calm. Blood pressure, pulse, and respiration all are reduced when in the presence of blue. Think of the calm induced by simply gazing out over the span of a crystal clear blue ocean or the brilliance of a cloudless blue sky.

The complementary color to blue flowers depends on the specific tonal value of the blue. True-blue flowers are best complemented using flowers that have a red-orange hue. Blueish-green flowers complement best to red flowers and blue-violet work well with orange as a compliment. There are so many blue flowers to choose from for any floral arrangement, and most can be easily grown in a garden or are readily available at a florist.

Hydrangeas, salvia's, tiny forget-me-nots, blue bells, and balloon flowers are but a few examples, but my all-time favorite for arrangements and for pressing are delphiniums. Delphiniums come in such a wide variety of blue and for pressing they are one flower that never seems to lose its color over time. I have some pressed floral art that is 30 years old and the blue delphiniums are just as blue today as when I first removed them from the press!

This longevity of color seems to hold true to all delphiniums no matter what their shade. I have also had good luck with all colors of larkspur and monkhood as well. I therefore try to include some of these flowers in most all my arrangements, as I know they hold up to the test of time.

Purple, lavender, violet, and indigo are the colors associated with the sixth chakra located on our forehead at the level of our third eye. It's no coincidence then that the colors associated with this chakra vibrate at high level of intensity opening up our spiritual awareness and intuition. Purple and the associated colors of lavender, violet and indigo have long been used to increase relaxation and reduce headaches; however, too much purple can make an arrangement feel too heavy and dense and is best balanced by yellow-green which helps to tone down its intensity. Deep purple is often associated with royalty, whereas the softer tones of violet and lavender often relate to a spiritual quality. The sixth chakra is all about evolved states of consciousness and the vibratory nature of this color reflects that.

The many varieties of lavender, salvia, delphinium, and monkshood are generally easy to find for any arrangement, but if creating a pressed floral design, some of the simple, easy varieties to press include pansies, violets, lobelia, and even azalea and rhododendron blossoms, which provide a varied source for sizes and shapes within this color spectrum.

As you consciously create an arrangement to fit a mood or attract a particular emotional state, it's important to know that white as a color contains all the wavelengths of visible light and therefore the entire color spectrum. The eye perceives the color white when light coming into our eyes stimulates all the three types of color-sensitive cone cells in equal amounts. White vibrates at the highest frequency of any of the colors. It is no coincidence then that our seventh chakra, or "crown" chakra located in the center of the top of our head, is associated with and vibrates to the color white.

White is the color most associated with purity and simplicity. Adding white flowers to an arrangement can help bring balance, contrast, and certainly interest to a design. A floral arrangement made entirely of white can be striking; however, white flowers once pressed generally do not retain the purity of their original color. The process of pressing a plant is to preserve its form and structure, not its color. Once the moisture from the flowers is removed during the pressing process, the reflection of light from which we perceived color is gone. This is especially true for the color white.

It has been demonstrated that in some blooms, color retention can be improved by speeding up the pressing process. Using silica-impregnated pressing pads or microwave ovens are two easy methods to remove the moisture. In the case of white flowers in particular, most artists often dust the pressed specimens with white chalk pastels to reintroduce color back to the bloom. Others use felt tip markers or specially created pressed flower dyes.

There are two schools of thought on dying flowers. Purists completely shun the idea, and the new generation of designers has found interesting and innovative ways to add color. When recreating wedding bouquets, it is very difficult to produce a design given the flowers most brides chose for their bouquet. Flowers such as roses, stephanotis, orchids, and lilies all contain a lot of moisture in their blooms and change dramatically once pressed. Designers recreating a wedding bouquet often must turn to tinting the pressed blooms. When creating a pressed arrangement, bits of white color here and there can be accomplished using Queen Anne's lace or baby's breath to add contrast and lightness to the design.

HEALING WITH COLOR

The natural evolution of using plants and flowers with specific color pigments to aide in healing originated from trying to replicate the corresponding colors formed by the rays of sunlight. This connection between color and its ability to have an effect on the body can actually be traced back to the first century A.D. when Aulus Cornelius Celsus, a Roman wrote the first known encyclopedia documenting a vast array of subjects from medicine and agriculture to military tactics. Of the many books he wrote, only *On Medicine* or *"De Medicina"* (Celsus) has survived intact. It is here, in the pharmacology writings, that Celsus first describes the value of using particular colored ointments to correspond with healing certain ailments in the body. Much of what Celsus wrote about disease was similar to homeopathic medicine of today, having its root in watching the way nature balanced and regulated symptoms rather than opposing them. One of his many gifts to medicine was observing and recording what is now commonly referred to as the cardinal signs of inflammation: warmth, swelling, and pain.

The art of healing advanced again when Avicenna (980–1037), a Persian philosopher, physician and disciple of Aristotle, wrote that color was an observable symptom of disease. He noted how color was an observable characteristic of particular bodily systems and how diseases could be healed by using flower remedies that corresponded to the color of the system that was out of balance. Avicenna was one of the first to write about this relationship between color and bodily systems developing a chart that he published in his *Canon of Medicine* (Avicenna), a five-book encyclopedia of medicine.

Avicenna was clear about including how important color was in the diagnosis and treatment of disease, relating it to both the human temperament and the physical state of the body. He believed that red moved the blood, blue or white cooled it, and yellow reduced pain and inflammation, and began prescribing potions of red flowers to cure blood disorders. Potions made from yellow flowers combined with morning sunlight were thought to cure disorders of the liver and digestive system. Over time the belief in using color to aid in healing evolved to include the shapes of flowers and plants, noting that similarities between these and the body parts they resembled could also be curative. For example, the plant eyebright, whose flowers look like bright blue eyes, and corn flowers are used to strengthen eyesight and cure conjunctivitis. A walnut, whose shape resembles that of a brain, is thought to be a cure for headaches. Skullcap, which has a flower that looks like a cap over a head, is considered an excellent remedy for nervous conditions.

In 1621 Jakob Boehme published *The Signature of All Things* (Boehme) documenting the relationship of the color and shapes of flowers and their correspondence to the human body. Now commonly referred to as "the doctrine of signature," its ideas correspond to the belief that nature uses colors and shapes to guide us towards the plants that can heal us. Nature exists for our benefit. Opening to this concept allows opportunity to view all life as being inter-connected. The energy that flows within us and in the natural world around us is all but the same.

This perspective of using plant "signatures" to determine remedies for particular organs and bodily systems is quite different from choosing specific colors for healing based on the vibrational frequencies created by the various color rays of the spectrum. When we talk about colors and their corresponding light wave vibrations, we are discussing the visual impact a particular color has on the nervous system, thus effecting energy flow and mood. Being aware of this allows one to create consciously by choosing colors that reflect a certain emotion or to create a desired mood. However, the theory that nature uses colors and shapes to guide us towards the plants that can heal us is well worth mentioning, as we are often attracted to what the body needs most.

Over time, mysticism and what some would call magical thinking was replaced by science and more rational thought. Reason dictated that all knowledge had to be certain. Intuition and the views of the spiritual and divine seemed to disappear and healing became a science focusing solely on the physical body, ignoring the mind and spirit as intrinsic parts of the whole. Interest in using color to heal disease declined. It wasn't until *1878* that the interest in using colored light for healing reappeared. Edwin Babbit's book ***The Principles of Light and Color*** returned to some of the early beliefs about color and vibration and expanded on these core principles to better explain how certain colors effect healing. He used color filters and minerals to increase the potency of water, claiming that the colored light raised the vibrational frequency of the water instilling it with additional healing powers.

The sheer numbers of research investigations he and others conducted and continue to conduct on color and its effect on the mind and body have yielded many positive results. Though Western science has been unable to verify the use of color to gain any specific effect, its practice and principles continue to gain popularity. In some cases, however, the use of certain colored lights has proven to consistently help with certain conditions. The vibrational frequency emitted by the use of blue lights helps the liver breakdown red blood cells counteracting the signs of jaundice in premature babies. Blue light is also used to improve the moods of those with seasonal disorders. This practice of using the benefits of colored light for healing is known as chromotherapy.

THE LANGUAGE OF COLOR

Flowers have always held special meaning for people. In Greek mythology, mystical meanings were attached to flowers and written about in many of the myths; however, it is worthwhile to mention that during the Victorian era in France, England, and America the giving of flowers took on the a very specific role of representing emotional sentiments that could not be spoken. Many dictionaries were published which listed specific flowers and their associated meanings. This was a secret language meant only for the sender and the receiver of the flowers.

Engaging in this form of communication gained its popularity in Europe after Lady Mary Montagu, the wife of the English ambassador to Turkey, published her observations about this cultural behavior that seemed particular to the women in the court of Istanbul. In her writings published under the title *The Turkish Embassy Letters* (Montagu), Lady Mary described how these women would wrap flowers or objects in a handkerchief to communicate with their lovers outside of their harem. The recipient of these items would then interpret the meaning of the message by selecting words that rhymed with what they had received (Montagu). For example, to represent the message of "do not despair" one might receive a pear. However, interpreting the meaning of a gift of flowers was often difficult to decipher.

With so many people having difficulty putting this form of language into practice it became necessary to have a more definitive dictionary to codify the language of flowers. The "Sur du language des fleurs" (Hammer-Purgstall), published by Baron Joseph von Hammer-Purgstall, was one such dictionary published during this time that stayed true to the tradition of using certain flowers in accordance with rhyming messages. The language of flowers, sometimes called "floriography" (Floriograpghy: The Language of Flowers in the Victorian Era), helped to transform the entire language of love into one that used flowers to speak the words of the heart.

As overseas trade exploded during the Victorian era, a great influx of new and exotic plants made their way to Europe and Britain. The Age of Reason and Enlightenment, which looked upon nature from a rational viewpoint, gave way to the Romantic Period stressing the expression of emotions, moral integrity, and passion. Many lacked the vocabulary and language to express what they were feeling and thus found it easier to adopt the symbolic use of flowers to describe their feelings while also allowing them to remain socially appropriate. The giving of an open rose would mean love openly, while a rose bud would best describe youthful love, innocent and fresh as in what a "bud" stands for. The white rose represented innocence and purity, and a white rose bud symbolized girlhood. Brides often select white roses for their bouquet for this reason. It was not unheard of to arrange entire bouquets flowers in a specific order to send an entire message. In society, women would wear small bouquets of flowers known as nosegays, posies, or tussie-mussies in their hair or on their bodice. This fashion accessory was known as a "talking bouquet" for the secret messages they held from the sender.

More often than not, the color of a particular flower became more important in defining its meaning. Consider, for example, what roses of different colors seem to "say." Receiving a yellow rose from someone you feel romantic towards may bring about feelings of disappointment. As was discussed previously regarding colors and emotions, red moves blood, which is pumped by the heart and in this way, red represents passions, the heart, and romance. The sunny disposition of the color yellow, on the other hand, is much more aligned to lightness and friendship. Further, the varying degrees of color in roses at times depend on their depth of color. The depth of passion and love, for example, seems to lessen as one moves from red to pink to white.

To sum up the usefulness of creating with color, the meaning of flowers and their specific colors is a unique aspect of symbolism you can use when creating, not only to enhance your own energetic flow, but also to send a special message to someone. The recognition of the beauty flowers bring into our lives has been with us for centuries. The flowers and plants in your home provide you with positive psychological payback. Think of them as part of your self-care and mental health treatment program. Be creative with your flower choices, and use color to inspire meaning into your designs as if the flowers themselves were your paintbrushes. Colors that fall near each other on the color wheel will complement each other and therefore be more calming, while the opposite effect occurs if the colors fall opposite each other on the wheel. Curvy shapes have generally been shown to be relaxing, while straight lines are, by design, more rigid and focused. Further information on these aspects of creating with flowers will be discussed in the design section.

Chapter Four

HEALING WITH SYMBOLS
AND SHAPES

USING SYMBOLS TO COMMUNICATE

From the earliest known records, civilizations documented their belief in the sacred nature of their world by using images and symbols to honor and connect their lives to that of the spirits. These symbols were formed by using the dot, the line, and the curve. Over time these elements evolved to form the circle, square, and triangle and created the basic foundation of the earliest forms of written language.

In the language of symbols, the dot was the first pictorial expression depicting a relationship between here and there. Whether there are two dots or many, the eye automatically creates an imaginary line from dot to dot forming a relationship between them. Primal man observing the rising and setting of the sun over a horizon depicted this event by connecting sunrise and sunset with a line in the shape of an arc representing the pattern of the sun's movement in the sky.

Primitive cultures gave meanings to these shapes and used them to communicate ideas. The circle evolved from the simple arc depicting the movement of the sun, which represented the constant movement of the universe as well as wholeness, one, and unity. Two overlapping circles illustrated the process of one dividing into two. This symbol of two circles overlapping also creates the primitive image of the fish-shape, which has become a symbolic reference to Christ in early Christianity.

Multiple evenly spaced overlapping circles arrange to form a pattern called the Flower of Life. This pattern begins with seven overlapping circles said to represent the seven days of creation. A close look at this pattern shows that it is also identical to what you would see in the cellular structure of an embryo in its third stage of division. It is said that the Flower of Life design can be found in every living thing that exists in our universe. (blog.world-mysteries.com)

The symbol of the square represents unity in the physical world since by definition any number multiplied by itself is a square. In ancient cultures, the square with its perfect symmetry came to symbolize the four primary orientations of north, south, east and west, as well as the four elements of earth, fire, air, and water necessary for creation. In the world of sacred geometry, the circle is the symbol of cosmic unity, while the square is the symbol of unity in the physical world. Given these associations, it is possible to understand that in some primitive cultures a square drawn inside a circle came to symbolize man's physical being.

With the circle representing the symbol for universal unity, and the square representing the symbol of man or the physical world, the symbol of the triangle took on the meaning of the element of air as well as the spirit of man. The triangle encased in a square and surrounded by a circle is the symbol primitive cultures used to represent the divine human and the trinity of the Father, Son, and Holy Spirit.

Over time a triangle with its three equal sides came to represent the concepts of past, present, and future as well as the mind, body, and spirit. A triangle with an upward point represents a strong foundation, stability, female energy, creativity, or ascension toward the spiritual world. Triangles pointing downward represent male energy, standing on its point awaiting penetration and descent into the physical world. (Frutiger)

The combination of the upward-pointing triangle overlapping the downward-pointing triangle forms the symbol, which has come to represent balance and divine union, or perfect balance of male and female energies. This shape is commonly recognized as the Star of David or the Seal of Solomon.

The spiral evolved from the basic elements of the line and curve. When circular arcs are drawn connecting the opposite corners of squares, the spiral shape begins to take form

(Hom). Due to its shape, the spiral came to represent anything that expands and contracts, such as life and death or the movement of consciousness. In the natural world, the Golden Spiral or the Fibonacci Spiral is created when a square is continually divided by multiple squares of decreasing size. The circular arcs connecting the opposite corner of each square begin to get smaller and smaller thus forming a spiral. This pattern is found over and over in nature and the universe and can be easily recognized in the shape of a rams horns, the inside of a human ear, a snail and nautilus shell, ferns before they open to a full frond, and the petals and leaves on flowering plants. The prevalence of the spiral in nature became a symbol representing movement either in the form of involution or evolution (Biedermann).

Many cultures used the spiral to create intricate patterns commonly seen in religious decoration. Design patterns using a single spiral evolved as multiple spirals were interlaced together to create detailed designs honoring nature and the universe. This interlacing of spiral patterns, known as the endless knot (Anna), can be seen in many of the early mosaics designs of eastern cultures tracing as far back as 2500 BCE as well as in the early Celtic Knot designs created by the Celts in Britain. In the purest form, the three intertwined spirals came to represent eternal life, its continuity, and life everlasting. However, over time this pattern came also to be known as a Celtic love knot, representing unending love and fidelity.

THE EFFECT OF SYMBOLS ON THE BRAIN

The human brain is built around the ability to identify patterns and attach meanings to them. It stores this information as images in the mind and responds with recognition when it sees something familiar. During human evolution, the brain's ability to process complex visual patterns became more sophisticated. In response, the brain grew in size to accommodate the need to store more information, thus allowing us to better survive the challenges of an ever-changing and complex world. Categorizing the stimuli which bombards us daily into patterns for storage allows it to be easily accessible when needed.

The question becomes: Do we connect to the visual beauty of a flower, or does our visual memory recognize and respond to the spiral patterns created by the flower's petals? Of course, not all flowers blossom with petals laid out in the sequence of a Fibonacci spiral, but flowers, as representations of nature's beauty, are symbols toward which the eye has an affinity.

The simple forms and symbols used by primitive cultures became the foundation for the first forms of expression and communication. Though most civilizations had their own unique characteristics, many of the basic elementary symbols were commonly understood by all. For example, human and animal figures, weapons such as arrows, the moon as a sickle shape, a mountain as a triangle, and water as a wavy line were all easily identified from culture to culture. Though the meanings varied slightly, the uses of these early shapes and symbols were easily recognized and understood.

Through evolution, many of these same symbols have been stored in our unconscious mind as part of a common experience still recognizable across all cultures and over generations. In Jungian psychology the innate ability we all have to recognize and understand the meaning of symbols is known as the collective unconscious (McLeod). It is a collection of memories of all human experiences from the beginning of time.

The symbols or *archetypes* that exist in the subconscious mind form the ideas or ways of thinking inherited from our culture, race, peer group, and family. They exist free from our conscious awareness. When a certain symbol is encountered, a message is sent to the subconscious and conscious minds eliciting varying responses. The subconscious mind is always receptive and suggestible, wielding influence over our life that we generally are not aware of; however, understanding our relationship to certain symbols can allow us to harness their effect on our brain.

THE HEART AS A SYMBOL FOR HEALING

A good example of a cultural archetype is the shape of a heart. The original pictorial shape is said to have evolved from the fig leaf, water lily, or the seed pod of the silphium plant used in ancient times as an herbal contraceptive (McDonnell). The shape resembled a woman's sexual organs and thus became associated with sex, and eventually love. By the Middle Ages, this shape became a metaphor and symbol of romantic love.

Regardless of the theories surrounding its origin, to the observer the eye immediately recognizes this shape and responds to it in an emotionally positive manner. Since love is a positive energy force, creating a floral design on a heart shape adds to the already powerful impact flowers have on the brain. The combination of these two elements creates a strong visual statement within the brain, generating waves of positive energy and feelings of well-being. This is why I call my pressed floral hearts "Healing Hearts."

Many students in my workshops have said that creating Healing Heart designs helped them overcome the pain of emotional or physical trauma. A Healing Heart design provides something tangible on which to focus as one is reminded of the powerful force of love. It does not matter whether the individual is conscious of what is happening or not. The brain recognizes and connects to the symbols of both the heart and the flowers stimulating an increase in the positive flow of energy through the brain.

Healing heart designs can also act as reminders of the joy people bring to the lives of others. To honor these individuals, I began designing Healing Hearts as a way to acknowledge the time and energy these special individuals devote to others. At the 1999 International Pressed Flower Art Society competition in Japan, I entered one of my Healing Hearts, winning The Chairman of the Japan Hana-Ippai Federation Prize. This award was especially meaningful because of what the "Hanna-ippai" movement represents to the country of Japan. In Japanese, *hana* means flower and *ippai* means a lot. Their mission statement emphasizes the importance of making communities more livable through natural floral beauty.

The Hana-ippai movement" began in 1955 after World War II, in Matsumoto City, in Nagano Prefecture (Hanna-Ippai, n.d.). The people of Matsumoto City decided to plant flowers as a way of healing the spirits of their people and to beautify their city after so much had been destroyed. The planting of the flowers was a great success, and the Hana-ippai Movement was formed as a means for the people of Japan to spread beauty throughout their country by planting flowers and helping heal the spirit of an entire nation.

In the United States, following the terrorist attacks on the World Trade Center on September 11, 2001, we witnessed the spirit of the American people rise from the ashes of devastation to become united in spirit. To honor that spirit, I created the design I call *Healing the Spirit of a Nation*. This became a sister design to my *Healing the Spirit of the World*, which I had the honor to present to Archbishop Desmond Tutu in 2000 at the People to

People International Conference in Hong Kong, acknowledging his lifelong effort in helping heal the spirit of the world.

The mind is naturally drawn to patterns and shapes that are harmonious in their design. When the eye experiences visual balance the mind, in turn, experiences a sense of balance and harmony, and brings with it a sense of well-being. When flowers are placed in a balanced floral arrangement, the eye detects visual harmony bringing calm to the mind. Flowers combined in arrangements with other positive visuals symbols such as a heart or Celtic knot design can add an additional impact to affect the visual image has on the brain, allowing calm and a sense of well-being to flow.

We need not spend great sums of money to receive the healing we seek. Creating floral designs and combining them with symbols that evoke positive imagery, whether conscious or not, will have a positive impact on the brain. Flowers, whether living, dried, pressed, or painted are powerful healers. The second half of this book will show you how to create the healing designs and allow you to experience an incomparable feeling of satisfaction when you see what happens next!

Part 2

FLOWERING
YOUR LIFE

Introduction

INCORPORATING FLOWERS INTO YOUR LIFE

Now that you have an awareness of the powerful effect flowers can have on improving your brain health and enhancing your emotional well-being, the next step is seeing how to incorporate flowers into your life. This chapter offers a few simple ideas to start you on the path to *Flowering Your Mind.*

Though all plants are wonders of nature, it is the beauty of the flower that has the greatest ability to affect our brains. The visual beauty of flowers stimulates blood flow in the brain, connecting us to the vital energy force that flows through our inner and outer world. Essentially, when we look at flowers, we are connecting to the creative force of life itself. As you begin to add flowers into your life, you might be surprised to discover how creative you really are!

HOW TO PURCHASE A BOUQUET THAT WILL LIFT YOUR EMOTIONS

Certainly, one of the easiest ways to bring flowers into your life is to purchase a bouquet at your local vendor. Following are a few tips to get the most from your purchase:

- Select blooms that have colors to match or lift your emotions. (Look back to Chapter 3 to read again about color.)

- Spend time arranging your blooms. As a creative exercise, engaging with your flowers stimulates more energy flow to your brain. Flower arranging can reduce stress, ease tension, stimulate your brain energy flow and in generally make you feel good as well as give you something beautiful to look at and enjoy. Arrangements that are visually balanced will help you feel balanced on the inside as well.

- Save money by purchasing a few flowering plants to group together in a pleasing display for your home or office. The effect of the blooms will improve your mood and work productivity.

PLANT A FLOWER GARDEN THAT STIMULATES WELL-BEING

The creative act of planting an outdoor flower garden can have a tremendous benefit on engaging many aspects of your brain to work together in harmony while providing a visual feast of color for your eyes. Follow these tips to get the most out of your planting experience:

- *Research the flowers that grow best in your planting zone.* The best flower garden designs incorporate several types of flowering plants. Before you plant, do your research. Choose flowers that perform well throughout the season so your garden is always in bloom with something interesting to catch your eye. If you're not certain what zone you live in or what flowers to select, consult your local nursery for assistance.

- *Create a focal point in your garden where your eye can rest.*

- *Work with year-round and seasonal interests.*

- *Use flowers that bloom at varying heights.*

- *Consider the flower's bloom time.*

- *Select a color scheme for your garden.* We have seen how color affects mood, so be sure to consider selecting complementary flowers and foliage when planting your garden. Find colors that visually suit your taste or consciously plant a garden with a color scheme to create a specific emotional response. An all-white garden, or variations of pink hues will be calming to the eye, whereas red flowers that are red, orange, and yellow are much more stimulating to the eye and the emotion. Consult a color wheel and see what colors you are most drawn to. For example, gardens planted in shades of the same color and hues are pleasing to the eye. Colors next to each other on the color wheel are also complementary, as are colors across from each other on the wheel. Once you select your color scheme, you can discover an abundance of choices within every color category for you to choose from.

- *Don't forget to consider foliage*, which can also provide the visual interest, texture and structure for your flowers to stand out.

EXPRESS YOUR CREATIVITY WITH FLOWERS IN OTHER ARTISTIC WAYS

If gardening is not your thing, or you are wondering what to do in the winter months while you wait for the warmer weather to return, try your talent at painting flowers, coloring pre-drawn flower designs, or actually creating a pressed floral arrangement using one of the templates in the back of the book.

All of these activities incorporate the principals already laid out in *Flowering Your Mind*. They all are methods of creating with flowers, which beyond being enjoyable will also engage your brain in healthy new ways of moving creative energy, increasing blood flow to the brain, and keeping the mind visually focused on a positive sensory stimuli.

- *Try your hand at coloring flowering designs.* Purchase one of the many flowering coloring books currently available. Remember to choose color selections from your pencils, crayons, or markers that complement your mood. Though coloring is an activity that is known to calm the mind and reduce stress, the designs you are coloring and the colors you choose have an effect on your brain. Try and make a conscious decision on what you are creating and how you would like your design to affect your mood.

- *Create your own pressed flower arrangement.* Creating pictures with flowers I have grown and pressed from my garden is one of my favorite ways to keep my special connection to flowers throughout the year. Not only do the flowers continuously delight and stimulate my brain, but remembering where a particular flower grew in my garden, or when I picked it for pressing provides me with memories that last for years to come.

Plants and flowers evolved on earth well before man came to inhabit the planet. Flowers enable plants to reproduce and facilitate pollination and fertilization. It's no wonder our brains become so stimulated at the sight of them since the sole purpose of a flower's color and shape is to attract pollinators. See what other creative ways you can think of to add flowers into your life.

Chapter Five

CREATING A FLOWER GARDEN

DESIGNING FOR HEALTH AND HARMONY

Planting a flower garden is a way to create your own private space allowing you to remove the stress of daily life and connect to the beauty of the flowers you have planted. Each flower in my garden has a story. I feel as if they are representations of various parts of myself, and spending time in my garden is like spending time with friends.

- *Understand the importance of planning, planting, and maintenance.* Gardens vary in purpose, size, style, and content. Planning, planting, and maintaining your garden can, at times, be more of an exercise of controlling and molding nature than anything else. Flower gardens create a visual display of color that will keep the brain entertained and stimulated. A garden is ever-changing, requiring you, the gardener, to provide guidance and a bit of discipline. Like writing, gardens must constantly be adjusted, corrected, and edited.

- *Create a focal point with meaning.* Good gardens have a plan directing the eye where to look. The temptation for many gardeners is often to add something just for the sake of growing it; however, once planted a new flower can often destroy the harmony of the line and color of the original garden design. Therefore, care should be exercised when adding new selections.

- *Use gardening to stimulate your brain.* The act of gardening engages hand-eye coordination as well as muscle memory that helps to ignite the brain's internal communication system. In order to provide the brain with a multi-sensory experience the gardener must also understand how shapes relate to one another as that is what provides the visual strength of the overall design. In this way, the process of designing a garden uses the same principles as one would use to arrange a group of pictures or furniture in a room. However, in choosing to design with flowers, whether in a garden, as a three dimensional arrangement, or as a pressed flower picture, the goal is to create a balance of harmony and a sense that there is a visual flow occurring between the shapes you are creating with and the space in which these shapes will be placed. The harmony between how shapes are placed and connected to their environment is said to be based on the ancient Chinese principles of yin and yang (positive and negative). In a garden, the plants are the shapes, or the positives, and the grass, walkways, or paving create the negatives.

In an upcoming discussion on the principles of flower design you will quickly learn that garden design is based on very similar concepts. Designing a garden allows you to control the view you want to create and allows you the freedom to decide how you want your brain stimulated. Remember, beyond the shape and flow of your garden design you must consider the colors you want and plant accordingly to achieve a constant array of complementary colored blossoms to stimulate your mood and emotional demeanor. Of course, practicality needs to be considered given that not everyone lives in a growing zone where they can garden year-round. For each growing zone, there is a vast array of specimens from which one can become familiar and choose.

GARDENING IN SMALL SPACES

Container gardening allows those who live in the city or have only a small outdoor space to use as a canvas the opportunity to play with colors and shapes while also having the advantage of portability. Following are a few tips on choosing and using pots and containers.

- *Choose pots and containers that create an overall collage of complementary shapes.* Unless a container is a work of art unto itself, try avoiding small containers in isolation. When grouped together, they make much more of a statement.

- *Choose containers that have interesting colors and textures to compliment the flowers you are planning to plant in them.* Just as it is important to focus on the color of the flowers you are using to stimulate a particular mood, understand the shape and style of your containers will be part of the mood or theme you want to create. Square-shaped wooden containers or period urns made of iron or cement reflect the mood and feel of an urban environment. Baskets, barrels, and terra cotta pots work well in creating a more rustic country theme.

BRINGING YOUR GARDEN INDOORS

Where I live on Cape Cod, I spend spring through autumn gardening outside. When the weather gets too cold to keep my plants outside, I bring my potted plants indoors. I spend the winter either buying flowers at my local florist to create an indoor arrangement or I design pressed floral pictures from the blooms I have gathered and pressed from my garden during the growing season. I continually am conscious of the powerful connection flowers have on the brain, which is why I choose them over most other mediums to create with. Also, by using flowers I have personally grown and preserved, each blossom provides me with a flood of memories about where each flower was grown along with when and where I picked it and put it into the press.

The success of the color scheme you choose for your garden will depend on the scale of your work. Start off with a simple framework of perhaps multiple varieties of flowers in the same color scheme. Mixing in too many colors, particularly in a small garden space, only ends up distracting the eye rather than giving it a place to rest.

Chapter Six

PRESERVING YOUR FLOWERS

CHOOSING YOUR METHOD OF PRESERVATION

Once you collect the flowers from your garden, you must decide whether you are going to create a fresh floral arrangement, air dry your flowers for use later, or press them to use in a picture or craft project. Each method has its advantages, depending on the intent of your end result. Fresh flowers, though beautiful, do not last long. During the growing season this may not be an issue because your garden is constantly providing you with new blooms every few day. In the winter, however, fresh flowers generally need to be purchased. This can become expensive if you are replacing flowers with fresh ones each week. For this reason, it is useful to try preserving some of the flowers from your garden during the spring and summer months when there is an abundance of varieties to choose from. This allows you to always keep your home filled with flowers without having to constantly purchase them.

Preserving your own flowers also creates wonderful sentimental memories when you look at them months later and remember when and where you picked them. I will say again that is does not matter whether the flowers are alive, dried, or pressed; the brain is still stimulated by the flower's visual image.

DRYING BY AIR VERSUS DESICCANTS

If you want to try your hand at drying flowers for use in a three-dimensional arrangement, you use the rustic method of simply gathering them up into a bunch to be tied with string and hung upside down in a warm dry room, or you can use a desiccant agent such as fine grain sand, borax, or silica gel crystals. Flowers contain moisture, so the more dense the flower blossom, the greater the degree of difficulty it is to remove that moisture. Unless you live in a warm, dry climate, air-drying flower specimens can meet with various levels of success. For this reason, I prefer to use silica gel as I think it offers the best and most consistent results. The downside of immersing your flowers into silica gels is that the petals can become so dry that they are almost brittle to the touch. Care must be taken in removing the specimens once they have dried so as not to tear the fragile petals.

DRYING IN A FLOWER PRESS

Because of my artwork, I spend most of my efforts preserving my flowers by pressing them to remove the moisture. Pressing flowers removes the moisture in the flower through pressure while also creating a two-dimensional specimen I can use in my designs. When I first started pressing, I used telephone books for pressing. Each day I collected so many specimens that this was economical. The naturally tissue-like paper was absorbent. With the extra weight created by piling books on top of each other, moisture from the specimens could be easily extracted. It was also a time when telephone books were readily available. Each year they were replaced by the most current issue, and I would collect discarded telephone books from family and friends. I always had more than enough phone books at my disposal.

During that time, more than *30* years ago, the science of pressing hadn't been as available as it is today. Though botanists have been pressing plant specimens for identification and classification for more than *100* years, the tools of their trade were simple. The standard was to place a specimen between two sheets of blotting paper, which was then sandwiched between two sheets of corrugated, cardboard. Multiple layers of cardboard, blotting paper, and specimens were stacked up to seven layers high and placed into a wooden press. The cardboard acted as a mechanism for air to flow between the layers, and pressure could be controlled by tightening wingnuts, which secured the press together.

Over the years I have had the opportunity to learn pressing methods from all over the word. In some countries the use of telephone books or wooden presses are still common, but as technology advanced the microwave gained favor as a way to remove the moisture in flowers quickly. Since it is not practical to put a telephone book in a microwave, nor is it possible to use a wooden flower press with metal wing nuts, new and innovative presses were designed. Some of these presses were quite simple. A flower specimen was placed between two pieces of blotting paper, which was then sandwiched between two sheets of glass held tightly tighter with rubber bands. Manufacturers produced microwave presses that were similar in design to the wooden press, but instead were made of heavy plastic and held together with plastic clips. Inside were soft sheets of felt and cotton to absorb the moisture. I even remember seeing a press made out of a cardboard oatmeal container. Wrapped around the outside of the container was a long sheet of felt held in place with Velcro. The limitation of using a microwave for pressing is the size of these presses. The presses can only hold a few blossoms at a time, making it difficult if you want to press many flowers of varying sizes at a single time.

It was the Japanese innovation of "pressing pads" impregnated with silica gel that truly advanced the art of pressing. I was first introduced to these pads when Nobuo Sugino, a master pressed floral artist from Japan, visited me. The International Pressed Flower Art Society, which he started in Japan, had a membership of 30,000 students, and it was the desire of this society to spread knowledge of this art to others around the world. During the late 90's, Nubuo Sugino traveled the world looking for the most innovative pressed floral art work. I was honored to be one of eight to represent the United States to be published in first edition of the International Pressed Flower Art Book, Vol. I (Tonttu).

I had already been a member of the Pressed Flower Guild of Great Britain for ten years, but had no idea what a popular art form pressed floral design was around the world! It was then easy to understand that in the pursuit of educating their members, the International Pressed Flower Art Society (IPFAS) wanted to create the best practice methods of pressing based on scientific principles. The pressing pads impregnated with silica gel not only fit into a standard wooden press, but the silica gel reduced the pressing time from three weeks to three days by being able to rapidly remove the moisture from the flowers. This rapid speed of pressing also helps keep the vibrant colors of the flowers. IPFAS was also responsible for creating and teaching its members an easy to use vacuum seal method for finished artwork, which would preserve the integrity of the flowers for years to come. I still get my pressing pads from IPFAS in Japan, and the Internet has made it easy to find desiccant paper from art preservation websites that can be used in place of blotting paper in a standard press.

Once my specimens are pressed and all the moisture has been extracted (flower petals should feel dry to the touch), I store them between sheets of wax paper in air-tight plastic containers. I always keep the desiccant packs that are found in shoe boxes, new hand bags, and even tech equipment, which I place into the storage containers to keep out any additional moisture. My storage containers are labeled by the color of the flowers inside. This allows me to easily select certain color themes when I start designing an arrangement, or if I want to create a certain mood.

There are many pressed flower books and internet sites with a wealth of information for those who want to start pressing flowers or enhance skills that you may already have. If you don't have the space to grow flowers, or the desire, but still want to create pressed flowers designs you can buy flowers already pressed on the internet as well. They come in many shape and sizes, as well as many colors.

My goal is to expose you to a variety of ways to incorporate flowers into your life rather than provide a lengthy discussion on which flowers to press. The greatest teacher is trial and error. Imagine the fun you'll have opening your press to see the results. One final note on pressing: if you are going to press flowers, start with flowers that are simple rather than ones that have a multi-petal blossom. These flowers contain a lot of moisture. Consequently, getting the pressure right to make certain all the moisture is removed can be frustrating for a beginner. Simple is better. Also, make certain you press enough material so that you have a variety of specimens to choose from when you begin to create.

Chapter Seven

DESIGNING A FLORAL ARRANGEMENT

PRINCIPLES OF FLOWER DESIGN

As you set out to begin creating your flower design, relax and begin to experiment with colors, textures, and shapes you have chosen. There is nothing better than hands-on experience. When we touch things and feel them, our brain immediately responds and seeks to make a connection. The visual connection we have to flowers triggers a happy response, which gets woven into your design pattern.

There are seven basic principles involved when seeking to create an appealing floral design. Since our brains are instinctively drawn to patterns and shapes, the success to creating a good design comes from incorporating the principles of balance, proportion, dominance, rhythm, contrast, harmony, and unity to ensure a beautiful outcome.

The line of an arrangement is either symmetrical or asymmetrical, but it is always balanced. The colors of your flowers and leaves, their shape and textures are what are used to create this balance in your design. You know your design is symmetrical if when you divide your arrangement down the middle both sides look the same. In an asymmetrical design, the two sides look different but the design is visually balanced by "weight" of the size and colors of your flowers. Balancing the visual elements requires you use flowers that are equal in shape and color to create a sense of harmony.

Proportion refers to the relative size and scale of the various elements you choose to place in your arrangement. Consider the size of your flowers to the relationship of the design. Large flowers have more visual weight than small flowers; however, small flowers can be grouped together to achieve the visual weight of a large flower. Light colors have less visual weight than dark colored flowers of the same size. It may take two or more light colored flowers to give the visual weight of one dark flower.

Every good floral design needs a center of interest. That which first attracts your attention to an arrangement is the element you choose to be dominant in your design. Examples of a dominant element can include a color, a contrast of colors, or a particular shape or object. The dominant element helps keep the eye focused on the design.

Once the eye is focused on the design it's important to keep it interested. Because the brain likes and naturally responds to patterns, it's important to create rhythm and movement in your design by regularly repeating some of your design elements. Repetition of similar flowers or leaves creates a path for the viewer's eye to move through the arrangement often taking a moment to rest on particular focal point. **Repeating visual elements such as flowers, colors, shapes, and textures not only creates rhythm but also helps to unify the arrangement.**

Contrast in an arrangement also helps to create visual interest. Contrast is created in a floral design by using opposite elements in your arrangement such as light and dark colors, rough and smooth textures, or large and small shapes. Colors that sit opposite each other on the color wheel can be combined to make a strong contrast.

Harmony is what brings together a composition. If your arrangement is composed of wavy lines and organic shapes, you would stay with those same types of lines and shapes.

Unity occurs when all of the elements of a piece combine to make a balanced, harmonious, complete *whole*. Unity is another hard-to-describe art term, but when it's present, your eye and brain are pleased to see it. When you are designing a visually balanced, harmonious arrangement, your brain will respond to the calm of the design as well provide you with a sense of well-being.

BUILDING A BASIC SYMMETRICAL DESIGN, STEP-BY-STEP

1. Pressed floral arrangements are built from the back forward. First, you must define the shape of the arrangement by laying out the background material in a balanced symmetrical design.

Using your container, decide the height and width of your arrangement. This will become the framework to guide the placement of the other flowers you will be adding. Plants that have long stems such as coral bells, lavender, salvia or baby's breath work well.

The first piece of plant material to be glued in place is the top center. Next, glue into place the right and left bottom pieces keeping them approximately parallel with the top of the container. The height and width of the arrangement is now defined. Fill in the remaining fan shape with corresponding pieces positioned at even intervals.

2. In the next step, following the pattern of the framework, select plant material that is completely different in size, shape, texture, and color. Use this to fill in any empty spaces. If you don't have enough of the same flower, you can alternate similar flowers to create a pattern of your choosing. Glue these flowers in place.

3. As the third layer is added, alternate your choice of flowers and plant material. At this point you should begin to see a symmetrical pattern begin to take shape. For this layer, either repeat the use of the plant material used in the framework, or select another complementary long-stemmed plant material. Again, if you do not have enough of a single variety of plant to complete this entire layer, create an alternating pattern with flowers that are similar to each other in color and shape. Glue them into place.

4. The fourth layer begins the development of the focal point of your arrangement. This is where you want to place your brightest and most interesting specimens to help draw the eye inward. Choose flowers with different shapes and textures from those used in any previous layer. Once you are satisfied with your selection, glue your flowers in place.

5. The fifth step continues to close in on the establishment of a focal point. This layer is going to frame the final specimen. A clear plastic graph ruler can help to ensure your flowers are evenly placed.

6. The final step is to glue the focal point into place. You can create the central focal point by either using a single flower or a few small flowers. The most important thing to completing an arrangement is that the design is unified, balanced, and interesting. It's fine to repeat the use of flowers previously used in another layer, or you can introduce a new flower whose color is complementary to the others in the arrangement. While variety of color, size, and texture of material is necessary to make an interesting arrangement, too much variety can cause the arrangement to look too busy.

GATHERING YOUR MATERIALS

Creating pressed flower arrangements is just one of many ways to add flowers to your life. If you would like to create a design by following one of the step-to-step instructions, you will need to gather your materials before starting. Whether you decide to press your own flowers or buy pressed flowers from one of the many internet sites, the plant material you have on hand to create will dictate how simple or complex your arrangement will be. Large arrangements require a large variety of flowers. For some of my more intricate and complex designs I must plan ahead almost a season in advance to make certain I have enough variety of pressed plant material. That said, even though the beginner heart design requires only a few flowers to be added to the template, the process of creating the design is equally as beneficial for the brain as the more complex designs.

- *Pressed Flowers.* Many books and websites can provide you with detailed instructions on how to press flowers. You can also purchase pressed flowers of all shapes, sizes, and colors on the internet.

- *Graphic design.* Decide on the design you want to work with and the desired finished size. Photocopy the design on card stock or other heavy paper. If you stay with standard paper sizes (5 x 7) (8 x 10) (11 x 14) it's easy to find a readymade frame to put your design in when it's complete.

- *Colored pencils.* These can be used to tint a black and white graphic to suit your preference.

- *Wax paper.* It can be helpful to lay a sheet of wax paper over the graphic illustration as you decide where you want to put your flowers. Once you determine your arrangement, you can slide the paper off to the side and use it as a guide to help remind you where the flowers go. When your design is complete, the wax paper can be used to cover and protect your arrangement until it's ready to be framed. *Do not substitute plastic wrap for wax paper. Plastic sets up static cling with the flowers. When you try to remove the wrap, the flowers will tear.*

- *Silicone glue or rubber cement.* This type of glue is used to attach the flowers to your design.

- *Tweezers.* Select appropriate tweezers to use to pick up the flowers.

- *Craft knife.* This type of knife is useful in moving the flowers into desired position.

- *Toothpicks.* Simple wood toothpicks can be used to put glue onto the backs of flowers.

- *Spray Acrylic.* This will coat the finished composition and protect it from moisture. To minimize fading over time, use spray with an ultraviolet blocker.

GENERAL INSTRUCTIONS FOR CREATING AN ARRANGEMENT

1. Copy or draw your template design onto card stock. If you copy the templates in this book make sure to enlarge them so your design will fit within the dimensions of a standard size picture frame. Keep your finished size in mind when copying the design onto card stock. Framing and craft shops stock a variety or pre-cut mats and frames for standard dimensions.

2. Set up a clean flat work space and gather all your working materials to the site.

3. If desired, tint the color of the graphic with colored pencils.

4. Lay out your floral material as shown in the step-by-step instructions for each design. You might want to take a piece of wax paper and lay it over the template. Once you find a balanced design, slide the wax paper off to the side and use it as a guide for placement when you start to glue into position.

5. Now you are ready to start gluing. You want to use a silicone or rubber-based glue. White glue has a water base and is not recommended for pressed flowers. Pick up your floral material with tweezers and apply a small dot of glue on the back of the flower. Use tweezers to position into place.

6. When your composition is complete it is time to spray coat and seal it with a few coats of clear acrylic spray. Create a spraying area in a well-ventilated space. Follow the instructions on the spray can. Apply two coats to seal.

7. When the acrylic sealer has dried completely, wrap your design in wax paper to protect the flowers from damage or moisture until you have it framed under glass. Never use plastic wrap as it creates static cling, which can stick and tear your flowers. Once framed, keep out of direct sunlight to help preserve the colors of the blooms.

HEART DESIGN

HEART DESIGN (beginner)

1. Copy the "heart" template onto a heavy weight paper. An 80lb weight (also known as cover stock or card stock) works best. Tint black & white graphic with colored pencils.

2. Build this arrangement up in layers from the back — forward. Keeping balance and proportion in mind, arrange small leaves around the heart. Glue into place.

3. Following the pattern created by the balanced placement of the background foliage, place your flowers onto the heart. Glue into place.

HEART DESIGN (intermediate)

1. Interested in adding a bit more color and depth of your design? This Intermediate heart design has only one additional step from the beginner's heart, yet it the end design result looks so completely different. Play around using your own flowers, or follow the instructions using the suggested material.

2. Assemble your material. This design uses tendrils I cut from a wild grape vine, but any kind of plant material that has a curve to it will help add grace and flow to your design. The rose buds were purchased on the Internet, and two Queen Anne's lace flowers picked from the roadside and pressed have been cut into quarters.

3. Working from the background forward. Arrange the tendrils to rest evenly and balanced along the outside periphery of the heart. Place a bit of glue on a toothpick to coat tendril. Press into place.

4. Cut the Queen Anne's lace flower into quarters. Glue into place.

5. Place the rosebuds evenly and in a balanced design onto the heart. Glue into place.

TOPIARY DESIGN

Once you have mastered how to layer the flowers and glue them successsssfully into place you are ready to advance your skills to an intermediate level design. Follow the instructions below either using your own pressed flowers or flowers purchased online.

1. Copy the topiary template onto a heavy weight paper. An 80lb weight (also known as cover stock or card stock) works best. *If your paper is not heavy enough the weight of the glued flowers will cause the paper to wrinkle.*

2. Evenly cover the topiary circle with Queen Anne's Lace. Depending on the size of your flower, you may need only one flower, or a grouping of 3 or 4 arranged together.

3. Keeping balance and proportion in mind, arrange small flowers evenly around the topiary circle. Glue into place. The design is now complete. If you would like to add a bit more visual interest to your design you can move onto step 4.

4. Select small leaves that are proportionate to the flowers you are using. Evenly place the leaves in a symmetrical design around the topiary circle. Glue into place.

BASKET DESIGN (Advanced)

This advanced design is easy to create. Make sure you have enough plant material of as this design uses more materials.

1. Copy the basket template onto a heavy weight paper. An 80lb weight (also known as cover stock or card stock) works best.

2. Beginning from the back layer and moving forward Arrange your first layer of flowers in an even semi-circle around the basket. The design should create a "fan" shape. Glue into place.

3. Following the semicircular pattern created by the background flowers begin to put into place your second layer. This plant material should be placed just slightly below the first layer. Glue into place.

4. Continuing to follow the fan shape arrange your third layer of flowers following the semi-circular pattern of steps *1* & *2*. Use two additional flowers to begin to build the focal point of the arrangement. It's important to keeping continuity and balance with the variety of flower choices you use in any one arrangement. Too many flower choices can make a small arrangement like this look too busy. Remember, the eye needs a balanced place to rest. Glue into place.

5. Fill in any remaining empty space repeating the use of flowers from the background layer. This will give your design depth and perspective. Glue into place.

Part 3

COLORING YOUR WORLD

Chapter Eight

MAXIMIZE YOUR CREATIVE POTENTIAL

There may be times when gardening or flower arranging is not practical and yet you may want to keep your mind positively stimulated. For those times, you can continue to *Flower Your Mind* by simply coloring flower designs which are readily accessible nowadays in the adult coloring book section of your local bookstore.

As we have discussed, it doesn't matter whether you garden, arrange flowers, paint flowers, or color flowers, when the eye perceives a flower, in any form, the brain is flooded with positive stimuli. Coloring flower designs requires the use of hand-eye coordination and fine motor skills. Activating these centers in the brain helps to stimulate the brain to work in unison. When the hands and the brain are required to work together on a creative project, it helps us stay present to the moment while blocking out any stressful thoughts.

Coloring can also be used as a meditative technique. For centuries, the Indian and Tibetan religions have been creating and coloring mandalas as a way to quiet the mind and focus on being in the moment. Allow your creative process to unfold by consciously selecting a color scheme to reflect or enhance your mood. Then, put on some music and get ready to improve your cognitive function by simply engaging in the joy of creating!

BIBLIOGRAPHY

About Flowers.com. 26 July 2004. <www.aboutflowers.com/workplace/research.htm>.

Anna, Christina. *en.m.wikipedia.org.* 14 May 2014. internet. 25 February 2017.

Augustin, Sally. "The Mental Health Benefits of Flowers (photos)." *Huffington Post* 1 April 2013. web. 1 July 2016. <www.huffingtonpost.com/sally-augustin/health-benefits-flowers_b_2992014.html>.

Avicenna. *Canon of Medicine.* New York: AMS Press Inc., 1930.

Biedermann, Hans. *Dictionary of Symbolism.* New York: Penguin Books, 1994.

Biophilia Hypothesis. 2016. <en.m.wikipedia.org>.

Boehme, Jacob. *The Signature of All Things.* London: J.M. Dent and Sons Ltd, 1912.

Bringslimark, Tina and Terry Hartig, Grete Patil. "The Psychological benefits of indoor plants: A critical Review of the experimental literature." *Journal of Enviromental Psychology* 29.No. 4 (2009): 422-433. <http://www.sciencedirect.com/science/article/pii/S027244409000413>.

Buhner, Stephen Harrod. *The Secret Teachings of Plants.* Rochester: Bear, 2004.

BUPA. 26 July 2004. <www.bupa.co.uk/health_information/html/healthy_living/senior/gardening/heal.html>.

Candace Pert, Ph.D. *Molecules of Emotion.* New york: Simon and Schuster, 1999.

Celsus, Aulus Cornelius. *en.,.wikipedia.org.* 1478.

Chiazzari, Suzy. *Flowers and Color as a Healing Tool.* 2004. <www.positivehealth.com/permit/articles/flowers%20Essences/chiaz53.htm>.

Clare G. Harvey, Amanda Cochrane. *The Healing Spirits of Plants*. New York: Sterling
    Publishing, 2001.

Colour Therapy Healing. 24 July 2001. <www.colortherapyhealing.com/nature/>.

Cowan, Eliot. *Plant Spirit Medicine*. Columbus, North Carolina: Swan and Raven Co., 1995.

Enchanted Mind. 26 December 1998. 2001. <enchantedmind.com/html/emotion/htm>.

Eva C. Worden, Theodora M. Frohne, Jessica Sullivan. "Horticultural Therapy." 2004.
    <edis.ifas.ufl.edu>.

Floriorapghy: The Language of Flowers in the Victorian Era. 9 August 2011. 2016.
    <www.proflowers.com/blog/floriography-language-flowers-victorian-era>.

Florists, Society of American. *flowers=happiness*. 22 September 2000.
    <www.aboutflowers.com/happier.html>.

Ford-Martin, Paula. "The Gale Encyclopedia of Alternative Medicine: Color Therapy." 24
    July 2002. *findarticles.com*.
    <www.findarticles.com/cf_dls/g2603/0002/2603000292/p1/article,jhtml>.

Fromm, Eric. *The Heart of Man*. Harper and Row, 1964.

Frutiger, Adrain. *Signs and Symbols. Their Design and Meaning*. New York: Van Nostrand
    Reinhold, 1989. book.

Gene D. Cohen, MD, Ph.D. *The Creative age: Awakening Human Potential in the Second Haldf of Life*.
    New york: William Morrow Paperbacks, 2001.

Goin, Linda. *The Element of Color*. 2 December 2001.
    <www.graphicdesinbasics.com/article1004.html>.

Hammer-Purgstall, Baron Joseph von. "Sur le language des fleurs." *Fundgruben des Orients,
    Volume 1 1809*: 32-42. magazine.

Hanna-Ippai. n.d.

Haviland-Jones, Jeannette. "An Enviromental Approach to Positive Emotin: Flowers."
    Evolutionary Psychology 3.1 (2005).

Hioe, Shirai. *Studies on Current Ideas of Green Space Conservation in Cities.* 25 July 1976.
    <iss.ndl.go.jp>.

Hirata, Dr. Koichi. *Efficacy of Oshibana Therapy* NHK TV. Tokoyo, 2001. Television
    Documentary.

Hoffman, lina. *The Psychology of Color.* 28 April 2002.
    <www.decoratingstudio.com/archives/physccolorarticle/phycofcolorarticle>.

Hom, Elaine J. *What is the Fibonacci Sequence?* 14 June 2013. <www.livescience.com>.

Honeywell, E.R. *Priciples of Flower Arrangement.* Lafayette: Perdue University, 1958.

Jeanette Haviland-Jones, Ph.D. *Exclamations online flowers.* 2001.

Jeannette Haviland-Jones, Ph.D. *The Flowers & Seniors Study Research Methodology.* 2001.

McDonnell, keelin. *www.sate.com.* 15 feburary 2006. internet. 26 february 2017.

McLeod, Saul. *Carl Jung.* 2014.

Montagu, Lady May Wortley. *The Turkish Embassy Letters.* London: Virago Press, 1994.

Nightengale, Florence. *Notes on Nursing.* New York: D. Appleton and Company, 1860.

Patil, Biorn Grinde and Grete Grndal. "Biophillia: Does Visual Contact with Nature Impact
    on Health and Well-Being?" *International Journal of Enviromental Research and Public Health*
    (2009): 2332-2343. 1 July 2016. <www.ncbi.nlm.nih.gov/pmc/articles/PMC2760412>.

Paul Nussbaum, PH.D. *Brain Health and Wellness.* Tarentum, Pennsylvania: Word association
    Publishers, 2003.

Peter Tompkins, Christopher Bird. *The Secret Life of Plants.* New York: Harper and Row,
    1973.

Petrovska, Biljana Bauer. "Historical Review of Medicinal Plants' usage." *Pharmacognosy Review*
    Jan-Jun (2012): 1-5. <www.ncbi.nlm.nih.gov/pmc/articles/PMC3358962/>.

Pioneer Thinking. 15 July 2004. <www.pioneerthinking.com/flowerswellbeing.html>.

Potter, Mary. "Detecting Meaning in RSVP at 13 ms per picture." *Attention, Perception and
    Psychophysics* (2014): 270-279.

Powell, Claire. *The Meaning of Flowers*. Boulder, Colorado: Shambhala Publications, Inc., 1977.

Roly Russell, Anne D. Guerry, Patricia Balvanera, Rachelle K. Gould, Xavier Basurto, Kai M.A. Chan, Sarah Klain, Jordan Levine, Jordan Tam. "Humans and Nature: How Knowing and Experiencing Nature Affect Well-Being." *The Annual Review of Enviroment and Resources 38* (2013): 473-502. <http://environ.annualreview.org>.

S.Shibata, N. Suzuki. "Effects of an Indoor plant on Creative Task Performance." *Scandinavian Journal of Psychology* (2004): 373-81.

Seong-Hyun Park, Richard H. Mattson. "Effects of Flowering and Foliage Plants in Hospital Rooms on Patients Recovering from Abdominal Surgery." *hortTechnology 18* (2008): 563-568. May 2009.

Tama Duffy Day, FASID. *The Healing Use of Light and Color*. 1 February 2008. 2016. <www.healthcaredesignmagazine.com/print/article/healing-use-light-and-color>.

The Editors of Encyclopaedia Britannica. *Collective Unconsciuos*. n.d. <www.britannica.com>.

Tonttu, Nobuo. *International Pressed Flower Art Book Vol. I*. Nihon Vogue, 1997.

Truth Inside of You. 2014.

Ulrich, Rodger S. "A Theory of Supportive Design for Healthcare Facilities." *Journal of healthcare Interior Design* (1997): 97-107.

—. "View Through a Window May Influence Recovery from Surgery." *Science* 27 April 1984: p420.

Virgina Lohr, C. H. Pearson-Mims, G.K.Goodwin. "Impact of interior Plants on Human Stress and Productivity." *Journal of Enviromental Horticulture* (1996): 97-100.

Wikipedia Foundation, Inc. *Language of flowers*. 7 July 2016. <http://en.wikipedia.org/wiki/language_of_flowers>.

Wolchover, Natalie. *www.livescience.com*. 31 July 2012. internet. 12/23 december 2016.

Wood, Betty. *The Healing Power of Color*. Rochester, Vermont: Destiny Books, 1998.

About Flowers.com. 26 July 2004. <www.aboutflowers.com/workplace/research.htm>.

Augustin, Sally. "The Mental Health Benefits of Flowers (photos)." *Huffington Post* 1 April 2013. web. 1 July 2016. <www.huffingtonpost.com/sally-augustin/health-benefits-flowers_b_2992014.html>.

Avicenna. *Canon of Medicine*. New York: AMS Press Inc., 1930.

Biedermann, Hans. *Dictionary of Symbolism*. New York: Penguin Books, 1994.

Biophilia Hypothesis. 2016. <en.m.wikipedia.org>.

Boehme, Jacob. *The Signature of All Things*. London: J.M. Dent and Sons Ltd, 1912.

Bringslimark, Tina and Terry Hartig, Grete Patil. "The Psychological benefits of indoor plants: A critical Review of the experimental literature." *Journal of Enviromental Psychology* 29.No. 4 (2009): 422-433. <http: //www.sciencedirect.com/science/article/pii/S027244090000413>.

Buhner, Stephen Harrod. *The Secret Teachings of Plants*. Rochester: Bear, 2004.

BUPA. 26 July 2004. <www.bupa.co.uk/health_information/html/healthy_living/senior/gardening/heal.html>.

Candace Pert, Ph.D. *Molecules of Emotion*. New york: Simon and Schuster, 1999.

Celsus, Aulus Cornelius. *en.,.wikipedia.org*. 1478.

Chiazzari, Suzy. *Flowers and Color as a Healing Tool*. 2004. <www.positivehealth.com/permit/articles/flowers%20Essences/chiaz53.htm>.

Clare G. Harvey, Amanda Cochrane. *The Healing Spirits of Plants*. New York: Sterling Publishing, 2001.

Colour Therapy Healing. 24 July 2001. <www.colortherapyhealing.com/nature/>.

Cowan, Eliot. *Plant Spirit Medicine*. Columbus, North Carolina: Swan and Raven Co., 1995.

Enchanted Mind. 26 December 1998. 2001. <enchantedmind.com/html/emotion/htm>.

Eva C. Worden, Theodora M. Frohne, Jessica Sullivan. "Horticultural Therapy." 2004. <edis.ifas.ufl.edu>.

Floriograpghy: The Language of Flowers in the Victorian Era. 9 August 2011. 2016.
    <www.proflowers.com/blog/floriography-language-flowers-victorian-era>.

Florists, Society of American. *flowers=happiness.* 22 September 2000.
    <www.aboutflowers.com/happier.html>.

Ford-Martin, Paula. "The Gale Encyclopedia of Alternative Medicine: Color Therapy." 24
    July 2002. *findarticles.com.*
    <www.findarticles.com/cf_dls/g2603/0002/2603000292/p1/article.jhtml>.

Fromm, Eric. *The Heart of Man.* Harper and Row, 1964.

Gene D. Cohen, MD, Ph.D. *The Creative age: Awakening Human Potential in the Second Haldf of Life.*
    New york: William Morrow Paperbacks, 2001.

Goin, Linda. *The Element of Color.* 2 December 2001.
    <www.graphicdesinbasics.com/article1004.html>.

Hanna-Ippai. n.d.

Haviland-Jones, Jeannette. "An Enviromental Approach to Positive Emotin: Flowers."
    Evolutionary Psychology 3.1 (2005).

Hioe, Shirai. *Studies on Current Ideas of Green Space Conservation in Cities.* 25 July 1976.
    <iss.ndl.go.jp>.

Hirata, Dr. Koichi. *Efficacy of Oshibana Therapy* NHK TV. Tokoyo, 2001. Television
    Documentary.

Hoffman, lina. *The Psychology of Color.* 28 April 2002.
    <www.decoratingstudio.com/archives/physccolorarticle/phycofcolorarticle>.

Hom, Elaine J. *What is the Fibonacci Sequence?* 14 June 2013. <www.livescience.com>.

Honeywell, E.R. *Priciples of Flower Arrangement.* Lafayette: Perdue University, 1958.

Jeanette Haviland-Jones, Ph.D. *Exclamations online flowers.* 2001.

Jeannette Haviland-Jones, Ph.D. *The Flowers & Seniors Study Research Methodology.* 2001.

McLeod, Saul. *Carl Jung.* 2014.

Nightengale, Florence. *Notes on Nursing.* New York: D. Appleton and Company, 1860.

Patil, Biorn Grinde and Grete Grndal. "Biophillia: Does Visual Contact with Nature Impact on Health and Well-Being?" *International Journal of Enviromental Research and Public Health* (2009): 2332-2343. 1 July 2016. <www.ncbi.nlm.nih.gov/pmc/articles/PMC2760412>.

Paul Nussbaum, PH.D. *Brain Health and Wellness.* Tarentum, Pennsylvania: Word association Publishers, 2003.

Peter Tompkins, Christopher Bird. *The Secret Life of Plants.* New York: Harper & Row, 1973.

Petrovska, Biljana Bauer. "Historical Review of Medicinal Plants' usage." *Pharmacognosy Review* Jan-Jun (2012): 1-5. <www.ncbi.nlm.nih.gov/pmc/articles/PMC3358962/>.

Pioneer Thinking. 15 July 2004. <www.pioneerthinking.com/flowerswellbeing.html>.

Potter, Mary. "Detecting Meaning in RSVP at 13 ms per picture." *Attention, Perception & Psychophysics* (2014): 270-279.

Powell, Claire. *The Meaning of Flowers.* Boulder, Colorado: Shambhala Publications, Inc., 1977.

Roly Russell, Anne D. Guerry, Patricia Balvanera, Rachelle K. Gould, Xavier Basurto, Kai M.A. Chan, Sarah Klain, Jordan Levine, Jordan Tam. "Humans and Nature: How Knowing and Experiencing Nature Affect Well-Being." *The Annual Review of Enviroment and Resources* 38 (2013): 473-502. <http://environ.annualreview.org>.

S.Shibata, N. Suzuki. "Effects of an Indoor plant on Creative Task Performance." *Scandinavian Journal of Psychology* (2004): 373-81.

Seong-Hyun Park, Richard H. Mattson. "Effects of Flowering and Foliage Plants in Hospital Rooms on Patients Recovering from Abdominal Surgery." *hortTechnology* 18 (2008): 563-568. May 2009.

Tama Duffy Day, FASID. *The Healing Use of Light and Color.* 1 February 2008. 2016. <www.healthcaredesignmagazine.com/print/article/healing-use-light-and-color>.

The Editors of Encyclopaedia Britannica. *Collective Unconsciuos.* n.d. <www.britannica.com>.

Truth Inside of You. 2014.

Ulrich, Rodger S. "A Theory of Supportive Design for Healthcare Facilities." *Journal of healthcare Interior Design* (1997): 97-107.

—. "View Through a Window May Influence Recovery from Surgery." *Science* 27 April 1984: p420.

Virgina Lohr, C. H. Pearson-Mims, G.K.Goodwin. "Impact of interior Plants on Human Stress and Productivity." *Journal of Enviromental Horticulture* (1996): 97-100.

Wikipedia Foundation, Inc. *Language of flowers.* 7 July 2016. <http://en.wikipedia.org/wiki/language_of_flowers>.

Wood, Betty. *The Healing Power of Color.* Rochester, Vermont: Destiny Books, 1998.

ABOUT THE AUTHOR

Suzanne Faith

Suzanne Faith, RN is a Certified Dementia Professional and Psychiatric Nurse specializing in the management of Alzheimer's disease and related dementias. Long considered an expert in the fields of caregiving and dementia care, Suzanne's unique ability to comprehend the often complex needs arising from this diagnosis has helped guide thousands of families over the past 30 years. Her expertise has led to the development of numerous Alzheimer's and dementia-based curriculum aimed at training professionals.

Suzanne is also an award-winning pressed floral artist and illustrator. Her unique designs, which combine her pen & ink illustrations with flowers grown and pressed from her garden on Cape Cod, resulted from her exposure to various pressing techniques used around the world. For more than two decades, Suzanne maintained membership in the Pressed Flower Guild of Great Britain, The International Pressed Flower Art Society and World Wide Pressed Flower Guild. She has had the opportunity to travel around the world using her pressed floral techniques to bring joy through a medium that transcends the boundaries of language.

Flowers have long been known to heal the spirit in many ways. Suzanne's desire to connect individuals to the natural world around them has led to the creation of her book, *Flowering Your Mind*, so everyone can enjoy the benefits of improving brain health with flowers.

ABOUT THE ART

The cover design as well as the other illustrations in this book were all created by Suzanne. To see illustrations and other designs please go to www.natureofdesign.com

Made in the USA
Middletown, DE
27 April 2021

38521418R00049